H... HELPS OUT

Carmel Reilly
Jane Wallace-Mitchell

Rigby

www.Rigby.com
1-800-531-5015

Rigby Focus Forward

Published in 2006 by Nelson Australia Pty Ltd ACN: 058 280 149
A Cengage Learning company

1 2 3 4 5 6 7 8 374 14 13 12 11 10 09 08 07
Printed and bound in China

Harry Helps Out
ISBN-13   978-1-4190-3673-6
ISBN-10   1-4190-3673-4

Harry HELPS OUT

Carmel Reilly
Jane Wallace-Mitchell

Contents

Chapter 1

Mrs. Black

Harry lived next door to Mrs. Black.

Last Monday, when Harry walked
past her house,
Mrs. Black called out,
"Come in and have a drink, Harry."

But Harry did not want to go in.
He did not think they had anything
to talk about.

"No, thanks," he said.
"I have to get home now."

When Harry told his mom
about Mrs. Black, she said,
"Oh, Harry, Mrs. Black is very nice.
Talk to her one day,
and you will see."

Harry went to his room
to work on his computer.

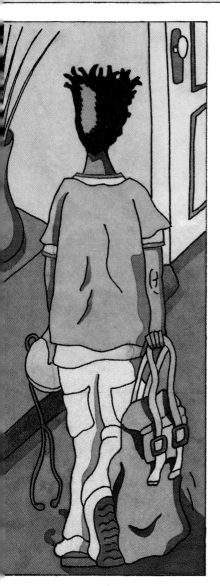

Chapter 2

Turning Around

The next day,
as Harry walked home from school,
he saw Mrs. Black outside
her house.

"Hello, Harry," she called out.

"Hello, Mrs. Black," he said
as he walked by.

8

Mrs. Black called out again.

"Harry, can you help me?" she said.

Harry did not want to talk to Mrs. Black, but he did not want to say no.

So he stopped and turned around.

Harry walked over to Mrs. Black.

"I think you are just the boy
to help me with this," she said
as she walked inside.

"What is it?" said Harry
as he walked in, too.

"With this," said Mrs. Black,
showing Harry a big box
that was sitting on a desk
in her back room.

11

Harry looked at the outside of the box.

"It's a computer," he said.

"Yes," said Mrs. Black.
"Your mom said that you use
your computer a lot for school.
Can you help me set up my computer?"

12

"Yes, I can!" said Harry
as he looked inside the box.

Chapter 3

Setting Up

Harry took the computer
out of the box.

He turned it on.
He got all the programs going.

In no time,
he had the computer set up.

"Can you work a computer,
Mrs. Black?" he said.

"Not really," she said.

"Do you want me to show you?"
said Harry.

"Yes, please," she said.

Now Harry goes over
to Mrs. Black's house a lot.

They have something
to eat and drink
and talk about computers.

Now Mrs. Black works on her computer
all the time.
Sometimes she is the one
who shows Harry what to do!